I0023176

F. Raymond Barker

Some Account Of Don Bosco And His Work

Gathered Chiefly From The Narrative Of Dr. Espiney

F. Raymond Barker

Some Account Of Don Bosco And His Work
Gathered Chiefly From The Narrative Of Dr. Espiney

ISBN/EAN: 9783742856753

Manufactured in Europe, USA, Canada, Australia, Japa

Cover: Foto ©Suzi / pixelio.de

Manufactured and distributed by brebook publishing software
(www.brebook.com)

F. Raymond Barker

Some Account Of Don Bosco And His Work

SOME ACCOUNT OF

DON BOSCO

And His Work

GATHERED CHIEFLY FROM THE NARRATIVE OF

DR. D'ESPINEY

BY

MRS. F. RAYMOND BARKER

Dublin

M. H. GILL AND SON

50 UPPER SACKVILLE STREET

1885

DON BOSCO.

———◆———

PARIS, in the month of May, 1883, witnessed one of those moral phenomena
which occur in every age—not excepting
this nineteenth century, with its spirit of
wary scepticism and keen examination
into the credentials of all that is, or that
is said to be, whether in heaven, on
earth, or in the bottomless abyss—it witnessed the children of this world doing
eager homage to one of the children of
light, *as such;* rich and poor, sickly and
strong, educated and ignorant, sufferers
and sinners, attracted in crowds around
the steps of one whom they regard as a
saint; the natural man doing conscious
and willing homage to the supernatural
life of grace.

When we consider that atheism and
agnosticism boast of Paris as being one
of their main centres, the thrill which,

like a magnetic current, ran through the
capital, when it learnt that Don Bosco
was in its midst for a short space, was
in itself a marvel. It was no renowned
name, no great powers of oratory which
exercised this strong and strange attraction: the simple hard-working Italian
priest of humble birth has no claim to
these; it was to the man of God, the
man of sanctity and self-sacrifice, of
faith and prayer, that all this homage
was paid, and whose benediction was
craved by the thousands pressing around
him, not only in the great churches of
St. Sulpice, the Madeleine, and St. Clo-
tilde, but also in the streets and public
thoroughfares of the city.

Don Bosco received, in a house of the
Rue Ville l'Evêque, at a fixed hour,
daily, those who wished to speak to him;
but, long before the time, the rooms,
staircase, and court, and even the street
outside, were crowded. Each person
took his turn : those who had not tickets
hoped at least to obtain a word or a
glance from the man of God as he
passed. Many waited for hours together,

on several successive days, before their
turn arrived; and while waiting, the
crowd recited the Rosary, the Litany,
and other prayers. This crowd was in
itself a touching spectacle; patient and
unselfish, it made way continually for
those who were sick or in evident afflic-
tion, and such as these came in great
numbers, to pass before their turn. In
the streets as in the churches, the one
or two Parisian clergy who accompanied
their guest almost forced a way for him
through the multitudes, while, as he
passed, those nearest knelt and kissed
his hands or his cassock. But the chief
beauty of this triumph was the perfect
simplicity and modesty of its object. It
is plain that the good priest takes nothing
of all this to himself, but refers it all to
God and Our Blessed Lady. He lets
himself be stopped at every step, listens
attentively to each speaker in turn, has
for each a distinct word of counsel, encouragement, or hope, and interests himself in the cares and anxieties of all. He
recommends great confidence in the intercession of Mary, Help of Christians,

and, in her name, asks alms for the many thousands of orphan boys he is clothing, feeding, housing, and teaching, in the hundred and sixty houses he has founded under her protection, and which he maintains solely by the aid of that Divine Providence in which he has such implicit trust, and which has never failed him. And it was to this Divine Providence that the people of Paris did homage in the person of its devoted servant and instrument, Don Bosco.

*
* *

The life of this holy priest is simple and uneventful, except as regards his great work, in which it has long been wholly absorbed.

*
* *

GIOVANNI BOSCO was born in 1815, at "I Becchi," a house and small property owned by his father, at Murialdo di Castelnuovo, about fifteen miles from Turin. He followed the occupation of a shepherd until the age of fifteen, when, in accordance with a desire he had felt from childhood, he began to study for the priesthood. He was ordained in 1841,

at the age of twenty-six. He was then
at the Institute of St. Francis of Assisi,
for the practical training of young priests,
and of which Don Cafasso, for whom he
had a great veneration, was Director.
Placing himself at the disposal of this
holy ecclesiastic, he was sent by him to
visit the prisons of Turin. Here he was
greatly shocked and distressed at the
large number of young boys he found
among the prisoners. These poor children, abandoned by their parents, and
brought up among the worst influences,
only became still more corrupted by
imprisonment with criminals older and
more hardened than themselves. From
this moment it became Don Bosco's
chief desire to devote himself in a special
manner to the poor homeless and friend-
less lads swarming in the back streets
and alleys of Turin.

He was pondering how to set about
the work he had in his mind, when Providence sent him an orphan, by way of
a beginning. He was vesting for Mass
on the 8th of December, 1841, the Feast

vagrant of sixteen, Bartolomeo Garelli
by name, attracted by the lights in the
church, came in, and wandered about,
gazing at the paintings and statues.
The sacristan, in want of a server, asked
the boy to serve the priest's Mass, and,
on his refusal, boxed his ears. Don
Bosco, hearing an outcry, hastened to
interfere, and after reproving the func-
tionary, began gently and kindly to
question the lad. He found him utterly
ignorant, and then and there began his
education, by teaching him how to make
the sign of the Cross. He took the boy
home with him, and bade him come for
instruction regularly every evening.
Very soon Garelli brought with him
some companions, chiefly masons' ap-
prentices, and in three months Don
Bosco's pupils amounted to a hundred.
By dint of patience he succeeded in
forming among them a choir, which
added greatly to the attraction of the
meetings.

The first place offered for these boys
to assemble in was the Institute of St.

name of "Oratory" to his work, to indicate that its life, its very existence, depended on prayer : he also, at the outset, placed it and himself under the immediate protection of *Our Lady, Help of Christians.*

In 1844, having completed his course of studies at the Institute of St. Francis of Assisi, Don Bosco was placed over the little Hospice of Santa Filomena, having also to attend to a Refuge for girls, founded by the Marchesa Giulia Barolo, and directed by a French priest, the Abbé Borel. Here, the only space in which he could assemble his boys—now 200 in number—consisted of a small room, a staircase, and a passage. On the other hand, he found in the Abbé Borel a man after his own heart, zealous and devoted, and who entered warmly into his work. But the two priests, who at once began to labour for the same end, could not suffice for the confessions; moreover, the number of boys coming daily to the evening classes continued to increase so rapidly that it was impossible, within these narrow limits, to

find room for them. Don Bosco, therefore, applied to Mgr. Franzoni, Archbishop of Turin, who highly approved of
his work, and induced the Marchesa
Barolo to let him have two rooms adjoining her House of Refuge. These
rooms he turned into a chapel. In one
of them was a portrait of St. Francis of
Sales, a saint whom he adopted as the
patron of his work, convinced that nothing but the tenderness and sweetness
by which he won souls to God could
influence and save these children. Hence-
forth his work took the name of the
Oratory of St. Francis of Sales, and his
assistants were called *Salesians*. Don
Bosco first said Mass in this extempo-
rised chapel, December 8th, 1844. Soon
he had 300 children around him, besides
many older youths, who came to the
evening schools, after the manual labour
in which they were engaged was over
for the day.

But now began the period of difficulties, trials, and opposition, and these
difficulties were neither few nor slight.
The work was to be sealed by the mark

of the cross. For some unexplained reason the Marchesa Barolo withdrew her loan of the two rooms, suddenly informing Don Bosco that he could not have them any longer, as they were wanted for some other purpose.

Aided by the archbishop, he obtained from the municipality the use of the long-abandoned church of San Martino dei Molini; but so ruinous was the condition of the building, that Mass could not be said in it: moreover, the only space for a playground was a small public square in front. However, there was no choice in the matter, and the Abbé Borel encouraged the children to make the best of it. " My boys," he said, " you know that cabbages, if they are to get a fine round head, must be transplanted; well, as we are transplanted, it is doubtless all for our good."

The good, however, was not very apparent. Three hundred boys cannot play without making a noise; the dwellers in the surrounding houses soon he informed Don Bosco that his tribe must remove elsewhere. Nevertheless, the syndic and municipality, who were by no means hostile to his work, next made over to him the church of San Pietro in Vincoli. To this church, which was in a suitable condition for the celebration of worship, was attached a spacious hall, well fitted for a school-room; there was also a large courtyard for a playground. Don Bosco was delighted; for nothing could be better adapted for his purpose. Alas! the very day after his installation in this desirable locality, an old rector, retired from active work, and living in the presbytery hard by, took alarm at the prospect of his tranquillity being disturbed, and wrote to the municipality in terms so strong, that the permission given to Don Bosco was withdrawn, and the children were all adrift again.

To squeeze 300 boys into his own little cell was a physical impossibility, consequently, for two months after this, their meetings took place in the open air. On Sundays and festivals the troop gathered early in the morning round the Father, who, like another Moses in the desert, led them to some church in the suburbs and said Mass for them. Each boy brought his morsel of provisions, and after a frugal but merry breakfast, an hour's catechetical instruction followed, then games of play, until Vespers. Often a long walk closed the day, and, in the evening, the happy and orderly band returned into the town, singing hymns and litanies, waiting, meanwhile, for their land of promise, in the form of some sort of shelter.

This existence, poetical, and in some ways, pleasant as it might be, in summer, became no longer possible as winter came on. Don Bosco, therefore, hired three rooms in the Casa Moretta, a house almost opposite the site now occupied by the splendid church of Our Lady, Help of Christians.

But fresh trials were in store for him. The Marquis de Cavour, at that time *vicario*, or chief of the municipal police of Turin, pretended to see in these harmless gatherings some occult political purpose, dangerous to the State. He announced his intention of suppressing them, and it required all Don Bosco's energy to avert the threatened ruin of his work. He met with no small opposition, moreover, from the secular clergy of Turin, who took alarm at the marvellous growth of this work, and declared that it would before long empty their churches.

The answer to this was very simple : almost all these children were strangers in the city ; most of them had no hearth nor home, and consequently belonged to no particular parish. Was it, then, any great harm to rescue them from the streets, and turn poor godless vagrants into orderly subjects and good Christians? This matter, therefore, was arranged without much difficulty. The next was more serious : the other tenants lodging in the Casa Moretta, where the boys assembled, complained so much of the crowds of children and the consequent noise, that the owner suddenly gave Don Bosco notice to quit in eight days : thus his work was again turned out of doors.

This was in the spring of 1846. The weather was fine, and as the good Father could not find a house in which he might gather together his children, he hired a field. " Our good God," he said, " will not treat his poor children worse than He treats the little birds." So primitive, this time, was the installation of the Oratory, that it brought to mind Our Blessed Lord, followed throughout Judea by his disciples, without a place wherein to lay his head.

On Sundays the boys, as usual, came early, and, before being taken to Mass, began the day with confession. The Father sat on a grassy mound, which served for chair, pulpit, and confessional. Passing his arm round the neck of the young penitent kneeling at his side, he heard each in turn in this simple and truly paternal fashion. Then, after Mass at the nearest church, all returned to the field for breakfast, after which Don Bosco instructed them in the catechism and on the Gospel for the day, enlivening his teaching with interesting stories delightfully told. The rest of the day was spent partly in religious exercises, the singing of cheerful *laudi* or sacred songs, and partly in merry games of play.

It was not long, however, before Don Bosco found himself turned out of even this poor field. The owner complained that the trampling of the children injured the roots of the grass, at the same time informing him that he could have the use of the field no longer.

And, as if this trial was not enough, he lost, at the same time, his post as Director of the Institution founded by the Marchesa Barolo, the remuneration attached to this being almost his only means of subsistence.

Considering the apparently hopeless state of his affairs, he was advised by his friends, including even the Abbé Borel, to give up the patronage of the children. "Keep about twenty of the smallest," they said, "and send away the rest. You cannot do what is impossible, and Divine Providence seems to show you plainly that It does not wish for your work."

"Divine Providence!" exclaimed Don

Bosco, raising his hands and eyes to heaven, "Divine Providence has sent me these poor children, and be assured that never will I send one of them away! I am perfectly certain that this same Providence will send me everything that is needful for them; and since nobody will let me *hire* a place where they can meet, I will *build* one, by the aid of Mary, Help of Christians! There we shall have room to take in all who come; workshops, where they will learn trades, courts and gardens for them to play in; we shall have a beautiful chapel and many priests!"

As he uttered these fervid words with flashing eyes, his friends shrugged their shoulders, believing that the poor priest was losing his reason, or had lost it already. Their belief was confirmed by the minuteness with which, when asked, he would describe the arrangements and dimensions of the future Oratory, his plans being out of all proportion to his means, present or prospective. One after another his friends dropped off, until he was deserted even by those on whose attachment he had most firmly relied.

This "monomania," as it was called, continuing to keep possession of his mind, it was resolved to "hinder him from doing anything which might bring ridicule upon his brother clergy," by shutting him up in a lunatic asylum. Accordingly, the superintendent of one of these institutions was spoken to on the subject, and was requested to let the poor man be treated gently, although, if need be, with firmness.

The one little difficulty, however, was to know *how* to get the patient in. Still, a couple of wise men could surely manage one crazy man: there need be no uneasiness on that head.

Two ecclesiastics arrived one day, in a close carriage, at Don Bosco's abode, alighted, and paid him a visit in his little room. They presently introduced the subject of the Salesian Oratory, which Don Bosco was to build. He spoke freely of his plans, and of the good results he should expect when they were carried out. The visitors exchanged a glance.

" Well, we must be going; we have a carriage at the door. Come with us for a drive; it will do you good."

Don Bosco was not in the least inclined to accept the invitation; however, as it was so affectionately pressed upon him, he ended by yielding.

" Get in, Don Bosco."

" After you, Rev. sirs, after you."

" No, no; we beg you to get in first."

" By no means! I know too well the respect due to you."

Impatient at so much ceremony, the two personages got in; when Don Bosco, instead of following their example, slammed the carriage door, and, in a stentorian voice, shouted to the coachman: "Ready! To the Establishment!"

The man had been told that he must start at the first signal. A vigorous lash set the horses off at full speed, and so they continued, the driver not being in the least surprised at the vociferations proceeding from within the vehicle, and of which he took not the slightest notice. The asylum was soon reached. Its gates, open in readiness, were closed the moment the carriage had driven safely inside. The head doctor was waiting, with a few warders, in the court. The gentlemen got out, very warm with shouting, and angry beyond expression.

"Come, come; calm yourselves," said the doctor. "I thought only one patient was coming, but we have plenty of room for two."

"What unheard-of insolence! Whom do you take us for? We are men of position, who will make you answerable to the law!"

"I see," calmly observed the doctor, "these men are both worse than I was led to expect." And he bade the assistants take them to their quarters, suggestively adding: "It may be necessary to try the *douche* and a strait waistcoat."

The unfortunate men were thunderstruck. Luckily for them, they knew the house-chaplain, and entreated to see him. The request being granted, he was able to testify to their identity, and get them set at liberty; but they had had a

narrow escape, and vowed, as they hastened from the premises, that, for nothing
in the world, would they find themselves
there again. Moreover, by this unlucky
exploit, they not only brought upon
themselves, with interest, the ridicule it
was intended to ward off, but they had
proved that if Don Bosco had indeed the
grand "folly of the Cross," he was also
not unprovided with a touch of that
" mother wit," which, on more than one
occasion, helped him to avoid the snares
laid to entrap him.

But time passed on, and the day came
when he and his troop of boys met for
the last time in their beloved field. It
was to be given up that evening, and no
other place for them had yet been found.
Don Bosco was pale and unusually de-
pressed. His face bore traces of bitter
tears. His children saw him fall pros-
trate on the ground and pray: "My
God! thy holy will be done! Wilt Thou
forsake these, thy poor orphans? Show
me what I must do to find a place for
them."

Scarcely had he ended his prayer when

a man—Pancrazio Soave by name—
crossed the field and accosted him:

"Is not your Reverence seeking some
place for your Oratory? My comrade,
Pinardi, has a famous shed to let; just
the thing you want. Will you come and
see for yourself?"

Don Bosco went at once. The shed
was primitive in the extreme, and the
roof so low that he feared it would be
useless. "My boys are not very tall,"
he said, "but still they are too tall for
this roof."

"Is that all?" said Pancrazio. "I
will dig out the soil as much as you like,
lay a good boarded floor, and you have
a palace! Besides, I am a choir-man,
and it will give me pleasure to help you
in the singing; and also, I have a beautiful lamp, which I will lend you for your
chapel."

Don Bosco was touched by so much
good-will. The bargain was concluded.
For the shed and the piece of ground in
which it stood he was to pay 350 francs
a year, and the shed was to be ready for
the following Sunday.

This being settled, Don Bosco went back for the last time to the field. It was evening, and a golden sunset lighted up the scene. The boys, when told of the shed of Valdocco, shouted for joy, and then, with their Father, all knelt and recited the Rosary, in fervent thanksgiving to God and Our Blessed Lady.

Pancrazio kept his word: all was ready at the time specified, and the archbishop having given immediate permission for the celebration there of the offices of divine worship, Holy Mass was for the first time said in this lowly shed on the 12th of April, 1846, being Easter Day. This spot, which, in its poverty, resembled the stable of Bethlehem, forms the site of the present Oratory of Valdocco.

It was not long before the number of boys who flocked to the new quarters amounted to seven hundred. The wonderful success attending the work not only brought back, one after another, friends who had withdrawn themselves, but also attracted others whose sympathy and assistance proved exceedingly valuable.

On Sundays and festivals the chapel
was open not only to the boys, but to
the inhabitants of that poor neighbour-
hood generally. The neighbours were
not slow in availing themselves of this
permission, and it was not long before a
marked improvement was noticeable in
this quarter, which until then was
known as one of the worst in the town.

The services, instructions, catechism,
&c., were all made so attractive in themselves, independently of the recreations
between times, that, when night came,
the boys were never willing to go away.
" Good-night, dear Father, good-night!
till Sunday! *Addio, a rivederci!*" But
by this time the good Father was so
wearied and worn out that he could
scarcely drag himself home to his little
lodging.

His evening schools, open on all week-
days, now became an established institution. Young men came to them in
such numbers that it was difficult to find
assistants enough to teach them. This
difficulty suggested to Don Bosco the
idea of forming his *Students.* Selecting

for this purpose the most promising of his youths, he undertook to give them a thoroughly good education, on condition that they, in turn, should undertake the office of professors to the others. This plan succeeded beyond all expectation. Don Bosco not only secured excellent and zealous assistants in his immediate work, but also many of these young men proved to have a vocation for the priesthood.

It would seem incredible (had it not become a fact so common) that the establishment, on a Christian basis, of evening classes for the instruction of poor boys, engaged all day in manual labour, should have aroused so much suspicion and antagonism as it did, from ministers of State, whose best interest it was to give them all possible encouragement; but so it was. Cavour again made a formidable opposition to the work, and would, doubtless, this time have succeeded in wholly suppressing the Salesian Oratory, had not an unlooked-for protector prevented this tyrannical act. Count Collegno, one of Charles

Albert's Privy Council, declared it to be the will of the king that Don Bosco should not be molested. Already the king had, on more than one occasion, given substantial proofs that he appreciated the work of the devoted priest. One New Year's Day, His Majesty sent him a gift of 300 francs, having first written on the envelope: "For Don Bosco's little rascals."

All this time the work of the Oratory, considerable as it was, did not interfere with the regular exercise of his ministry in the prisons. There, as was his wont, he occupied himself in a special manner with the large numbers of boys in confinement. These poor lads, for the most part, had been led into evil practices by hardened malefactors much older than themselves. The results of his pastoral care were often most consoling. After one of the retreats he had preached for them, almost the whole number went to Communion.

Rejoicing at the good dispositions of his dear prisoners, he resolved to procure for them a treat of some kind, and decided that nothing would be so good for them, or delight them half so much, as a day in the country.

He went straight to the governor of the prison, and, with perfect simplicity, made his request, as if it were the most natural thing in the world.

The governor was, for a moment, dumb with amazement. Like certain persons not long before, he doubted if the priest could be quite sane. "What!" he exclaimed; "do you imagine, Sir Priest, that the king's soldiers have not something else to do than take these fellows out for a walk? And are you not aware that I am responsible for every case of evasion?"

"But who, Illustrissimo Gubernatore, wants the king's soldiers, or a single man of them? I take the whole responsibility: there will be no case of evasion. I promise to bring faithfully back to you every one of the lads with whom you are so good as to trust me."

How this strange permission came to be granted was never known; but so it was—and this, too, after having been submitted to the notoriously anti-clerical minister, Ratazzi.

On the day fixed, directly after early Mass, the party set out: that is to say, three hundred and fifty boys and young men came out of prison in good order, led by Don Bosco, calm and smiling.

The royal castle of Stupinigi had been chosen as the end of the expedition : twelve miles or so out, and twelve to return, was not too much to unstiffen young limbs cramped by more or less long confinement. No words could paint the joy which beamed on every face. During the whole of that happy day there was not the shadow of anything disorderly, no mischief done, nor a single fruit stolen. The chief thought of all these lads was to keep a tender watch over their Father. They noticed that he looked fatigued, and in a moment loaded their own shoulders with the baskets of provisions, and made Don Bosco mount the ass which his thoughtfulness had provided in order to carry them, two of the boys persisting in walking by him to hold the bridle.

When, after returning to the town, the names were called over that night, the governor found that not a single prisoner was missing.

We learn, without surprise, that at one time Don Bosco could not walk in the streets of Turin without being immediately surrounded by children, and sometimes in such crowds as to impede the circulation.

Besides the prisons, Don Bosco regularly visited the Hospital Cottolengo; he also wrote various educational and devotional manuals for the use of the Oratory. In short, the amount of work which filled each day as it came, without any respite, was enormous. No health, however robust, could long resist such pressure. Don Bosco's strength suddenly and completely broke down, and the doctors insisted on his going into the country for rest.

But rest was not for him. His retreat was daily invaded by visits, both from his students and his boys; moreover, on Saturdays he went back into the town to

in order to assist at the Oratory of Valdocco. A severe cold, caught on one of
these occasions, brought his already ex-
hausted frame to the last extremity, and
the physicians gave up all hope of recovery.

One night, which seemed to be his
last, the Abbé Borel, who was watching
by his friend, said to him, authoritatively:
" Don Bosco, ask God to cure you."

The dying man refused. " No," he
said; " I give myself up entirely to his
will."

" But think of your children; you cannot leave them thus. For their sakes
ask the good God to restore you to
health."

Then Don Bosco murmured: " Yes, O
Lord, if this should be thy good pleasure,
let me recover. *Non recuso laborem !*"

"Victory!" exclaimed the Abbé. "Now
I am sure you will get well." And in
fact, from that night, the invalid began
to amend.

Then only was it known how his children loved him. It was found that nearly
all, in order to obtain his cure, had made

vows and undertaken penances so severe, that he was obliged to interpose his authority to commute a considerable number, and lessen almost all.

The extreme prostration in which his illness left him made three months of quiet absolutely necessary. He spent them in the home where he was born, I Becchi, near Murialdo di Castelnuovo, about fifteen miles from Turin. When the time came for returning, his excellent mother, Margherita, to whom he had spoken freely of his work, resolved to accompany him. She was a woman of warm and generous heart, simple and courageous : without hesitation she quitted the peaceful home she had never left since her marriage, to share the labours of the son she so greatly revered, and be a mother to his adopted family.

On the 3rd of November, 1846, mother and son set out from I Becchi on foot: the one carrying a breviary, the other a basket of provisions. As they were crossing the Rondo, not far from Turin, they met Don Vola, who had more hand in his schools and catechism classes.

"How tired you are, my poor friend!" he said, after the first greeting. "What are you going to do?"

"Settle at the Oratory. "I have taken rooms in Pinardi's house, close to the chapel."

"But you have no resources that I know of. How shall you manage?"

"I don't know in the least; I only know that God will provide."

"I have nothing but my watch," said Don Vola; "you must accept it as a nest-egg." And he put his watch into Don Bosco's hand, who took it as simply as it was given.

Next day the watch was sold to buy the necessary furniture for the empty rooms. Other payments were also urgent; there were so many children in need of food, of clothing, of everything but a good appetite; and then Don Bosco sold the vineyard and the few acres besides, which constituted all his own and his mother's worldly possessions. Madame Margherita sent for her wedding presents, still carefully preserved through all these years, her fine house-linen, and even her *corona*—the pearl ornaments which had been her wedding heirloom, the ornaments so precious to Italian women that they will suffer starvation before they will part with them. The choicest of these she gave to adorn the altar of Our Blessed Lady, and sold the rest.

This noble woman was soon joined by a group of charitable ladies, the first to set the example being the mother of the Archbishop of Turin. These women proved most zealous and unwearied co-operators in Don Bosco's work, and their aid in feeding and clothing his boys invaluable.

Being thus definitively installed at the Oratory, Don Bosco, early in 1847, laid down *Regulations* for his work. These regulations have since been adopted in many schools besides those attached to the Salesian Oratorians. He instituted *officers* among the boys, choosing for this purpose the most intelligent, pious, and trustworthy, and appointing to each a certain share of superintendence and responsibility. He also, to encourage them in piety, formed amongst them a "Company of St. Aloysius Gonzaga." This "Company" was approved by Mgr. Franzoni, who, moreover, to give a proof of his interest in the whole work, announced his intention of giving Confirmation to the children in the chapel of Valdocco. This, the "famous shed," was made as magnificent for the occasion as hangings and wreaths could make it. When the prelate mounted the little pulpit, he was obliged to take off his mitre to be able to stand upright, but his words none the less went to the hearts of his youthful and enthusiastic hearers.

It was about this time that Don Bosco, knowing that many poor boys who attended the classes had no fixed place to sleep in, but spent the night on doorsteps, or else in wretched lodgings, where the risks they ran were of a far more serious nature than those of exposure to cold or miasma, hired an empty hay-loft to serve as a dormitory for them. This loft he spread with plenty of clean straw, and all the blankets that could be spared; when blankets fell short, sacks took their place, and those only who have slept upon straw can properly appreciate these sacks. The sleeper gets inside, and in this way has an upper and an under sheet without further trouble.

This primitive dormitory or night-refuge proved of very great service; but Don Bosco had to find out by experience that all is not roses for providers of "ready furnished lodgings." As far as the children and lads were concerned, all went well; but one night the priest's hospitable heart ensnared him into housing a band of older vagrants he had met with in the waste lands about the Oratory. When morning came, he went betimes to say a few kind words to them, which might, he hoped, be profitable to their souls, but found the dormitory stripped and empty, his guests having made off with every blanket and every sack. This misadventure, however, far from discouraging Don Bosco, only incited him to do more than ever; con

sidering that the more little vagrants
could be rescued from vice, the fewer
there would be to grow up to practice
thieving.

In the month of May following, a poor
little orphan, a mason's apprentice, came
one evening to the door. He was wet
to the skin, his scanty rags being no
protection against the rain, which fell in
torrents; and for two days he had not
tasted food. Madame Margherita took
him in, made up the fire, warmed and
fed him, put on dry garments instead of
his dripping tatters, and arranged for
him a bed in the kitchen. He was the
first boarder of the Oratory. Soon there
came a second, and so on until there
were seven; then it was impossible to take
in more, for want of room. Room was
equally scarce where the boys had their
meetings; chapel and playground were
alike overcrowded: the number assembled often amounted to seven hundred,
and every place had grown too small.
Don Bosco and his faithful fellow-
worker, the Abbé Borel, took counsel
together as to what was to be done,

and decided that it was absolutely necessary to open a second Oratory.

After long search, Don Bosco found a tenement fairly suitable for his purpose. The landlady, however, asked a rent so out of proportion to the value of the house, that it was impossible to take it on her terms. In vain he requested her to reconsider her decision ; she was inflexible. During the discussion a storm had gathered, unperceived, as night came on, and suddenly a formidable peal of thunder burst directly overhead, shaking the house, and extinguishing the lamp which lighted the room, leaving it in darkness. The lady, almost beside herself with fear, changed her tone. "Dear and excellent Father, only ask of God that the lightning may not hurt me, and you shall have any terms you please !" Don Bosco said he prayed that God would watch over her now and always. The storm passed on its rapid way, and the worthy woman, enchanted, made no more difficulty about accepting a reasonable rent. This house, which was to become the new Oratory of St. Aloysius, being near the river Po, was in a quarter largely inhabited by washerwomen.

The Archbishop warmly encouraged the extension of Don Bosco's work : many of the secular clergy of Turin had learnt, instead of opposing it, to give it their cordial concurrence. Numerous lay persons, also, took great interest in the new foundation, gave the furniture for the chapel, the sacred vessels, &c., the vestments for Holy Mass and benediction being embroidered by different ladies. The new Oratory was solemnly opened on the 8th of December, 1847, the same Feast of Our Lady on which, six years before, Don Bosco had picked up his first orphan vagrant. In these six years, in spite of all human opposition, his work had marvellously prospered, for "the hand of the Lord was with him," and that first "little one" had indeed "become a thousand."

Encouraged by their Archbishop, several of the clergy of Turin gladly offered their assistance, and, under the direction of the Abbé Morel, undertook the functions of chaplains or professors, an arrangement which lasted until the Oratory of St. Francis of Sales had had time to provide itself with priests trained in its midst. Then, the latter definitively took the direction of the house.

Don Eosco, meantime, remained actively engaged in his work at the Valdocco, and there established the custom, invariably observed ever since, in the Salesian Institutions, of giving a little address by way of closing the day. These addresses never lasted much longer than ten minutes, and were as simple as possible. He tried to give the boys each time only one distinct idea, but this he managed so to bring home to them that they rarely forgot it. Many afterwards spoke of these evening words as having been the turning-point in their lives. Don Bosco's earnest desire to provide a permanent abode for homeless boys had, as we have seen, begun, but only begun, to be realised. The price Pinardi asked for his house was 80,000 francs (£3,200)—a price impossible for him to give: he could only hire room after room as it was left vacant by departing lodgers, until, by dint of untold efforts, he contrived to board and lodge fifteen fortunate waifs.

Besides these, he took in, for meals only, fifty boys, who worked in Turin and slept at their own homes; but these meals were made the opportunities for many a kind and helpful word to his young guests. As their numbers increased, he received them by fifties, week by week in turns: a plan which, while extending the limits of his help and influence, immensely increased the amount of work falling on his mother, as well as himself.

While the good Margherita was cooking, or patching and darning, Don Bosco might be often seen sweeping the house, sawing wood, drawing water from the well, or peeling vegetables, or even sewing up, with less elegance than solidity, some formidable rent in the garments of a juvenile wearer. Nor did he disdain, in case of need, to gird on an apron and prepare the *polenta*, which, on such occasions, was always pronounced to be exceptionally delicious.

The refectory was elementary in the extreme. Everyone sat where he could, some on the floor, Eastern fashion; some on logs of wood in the court-yard; others on the stairs; all the same, bowls and platters emptied as if by magic, and were then at once carried to the spring, washed, and put by; the spoon being carefully restored to the owner's pocket.

And besides this spring, at which the boys quenched their thirst, there was also a spring of youthfulness of spirit, ever fresh and pure, in the heart of Don Bosco, which made these primitive repasts delightful to all who shared them. No one knows better than he how to interest the young, and, without their even suspecting it, to instruct, encourage and strengthen them in all that is earnest, high-minded, and good. His delightful stories made the dinner-hour one of the happiest of the day, and any want of solidity in the repast was compensated for by its gaiety. The *menu* consisting, however, of an invariable alternation of soup and bread, bread and soup—the same for Don Bosco as for his boys—it more than once happened that ecclesiastics who had offered their assistance found themselves obliged to withdraw it, being unable to sustain nature on so meagre a diet.

The sweet voices remarked by Don Bosco among the children, led him early to encourage them in the cultivation of music, both vocal and instrumental, especially in the evening schools. Many excellent organists and professors have already been formed among the pupils. The remarkable success of these schools led the municipality of Turin to award to Don Bosco the sum of 6,000 francs, and afterwards another thousand as a prize for music. At the same time, it decreed a yearly sum of money in aid of his works. This sum he received until 1872.

About the same time, the Archbishop of Turin, who, from the first, had never hesitated in his cordial support of Don Bosco, now regularly conferred upon him the necessary powers for performing in the church of the Salesian oratories all the functions to which parochial churches have a right, and thus the Oratory became, as the prelate was pleased to call it, " The Parish of Outcast Children."

Still, together with these successes, Don Bosco had to contend against a certain amount of opposition, sometimes from unexpected quarters. Moreover, he was pursued by the relentless hatred of the sects—secret societies, Freemasons, and Socialists; these, together with persons of evil lives, were irritated beyond measure at his reclaiming and Christianizing localities of which they had hitherto had undisturbed possession.

One day, when Don Bosco was in the chapel of Valdocco, surrounded by the children, whom he was catechising, he was shot at by some miscreant through an open window. The bullet passed through his cassock, between the arm and the breast, and flattened itself against the wall. The boys, whose singing was suddenly stopped by the report, rushed in alarm to the Father, who stood unmoved and smiling.

had not thrown him out of time, he would have hit me: but he is no musician!" Then, looking at the hole in his cassock, he lamented that this should have been damaged, since, old as it was, it was his only one.

Being once sent for late at night, to administer the Last Sacraments to a poor woman, he was taken to a house some distance off; two or three of his elder lads had insisted on going with him and waiting outside. On entering the sick-room, he found four men, armed with stout sticks, round the bed, while the person within it looked neither feminine nor dying. The solitary candle was suddenly thrown down and extinguished; Don Bosco seized a chair, and, with it, shielded his head from the blows by which he was now assailed on all sides. Profiting by the darkness, he groped his way to the door, and in another minute was walking home with his companions, leaving the men to belabour one another until they found out their mistake.

In the early days of the Oratory, the

Valdocco quarter was not populous, as now; the houses were far apart, and a tract of waste land and brushwood separated the Oratory from the last habitations of the town. One evening, when Don Bosco was returning home after dark, and had begun to cross this lonesome tract, he suddenly saw by his side an enormous grey dog. A first feeling of alarm was removed by the gentleness of the splendid creature, which, after gambolling round him, walked quietly by his side until it saw him safely indoors. From this time, when Don Bosco had been detained in Turin until after dusk, he was joined almost invariably, as soon as he had left the town, by his four-footed friend, whom, on account of his colour, he called *Il Grigio*, and so accompanied to the Oratory door.

On several occasions this dog saved his life. He was one night returning home by the road leading from La Consolata to the Hospital Cottolengo, when, at a certain lonely spot, two men rushed upon him. one of whom threw a cloak over his head. Don Bosco, half-suffocated, gave himself up for lost. At the same moment, a fierce yell resounded close at hand, and *Il Grigio*, springing on the assailant, seized him by the throat, and had him down in an instant, the other making off with all speed. He was soon followed by his fellow-assassin, when Don Bosco, in answer to his cries for mercy, called the dog off, and went on his way, attended by his deliverer.

Another evening, as he returned by the Corso San Massimo, a man fired two shots at him, scarcely at arm's length, from behind a tree; but each time the pistol missed fire. The murderer then fell upon him with some surer weapon, when Grigio bounded on the scene, flew upon the man, and held him until Don Bosco bade him leave go, when the fellow was glad to escape with his life.

Not long afterwards, a number of assassins seem to have banded together, in order to make sure of their victim. Don Bosco had one night taken the lonely road leading from the Place Emanuele Filiberto to the Rondo, when, perceiving that he was followed, he quickened his steps. Presently, a man came up, prepared to fell him with a heavy club. As he brandished it in the air, Don Bosco, turning quickly round, gave the fellow a blow which sent him rolling in the dust; but at the same moment, other men, similarly armed, issued on all sides from the bushes where they lay concealed. Resistance was impossible; suddenly, however, a terrific roar announced the arrival of *Il Grigio*. Swift as thought, the noble creature bounded round and round the priest, barking furiously, and showing such formidable fangs that not a single miscreant dared come near him : the whole gang beat an ignominious retreat, and the dog escorted Don Bosco safely home.

On another occasion, the latter was preparing to go out after dark; his mother endeavouring to dissuade him from his purpose, but without success. On opening the door, there lay Grigio along the threshold, and showing no in-

"Come, my good fellow, let me pass!"
said the priest, pushing him gently with
his foot. But the dog, usually so docile,
growled ominously, and refused.

"You see, my son," said Madame
Margherita, "the dog is wiser than you
are: be advised by him, and stay."

After two more attempts, Don Bosco,
finding it waste of time to argue with
Grigio, quietly went back to his room.
A quarter of an hour afterwards, a neighbour came in all haste to beg Don Bosco
not to go out for any reason soever,
as he had seen a number of ruffians con-
gregated in a narrow alley, and had
learned that they were resolved, this time,
to have his life at any price.

One evening, Grigio made his appear-
ance in the playground of the Oratory.
"Oh, here is Don Bosco's dog!" exclaimed one of the youths, and the children, at first inclined to be shy of this
new acquaintance, now hailed him as a
playfellow: some mounted his back,
some stroked his silken ears, and they
took him thus to the refectory, where Don
Bosco and his mother, with several priests,

were at supper. "Here is my Grigio!" he said, and the dog came to be caressed, but refused everything that was offered him to eat, and ended by laying his magnificent head on the edge of the table and looking affectionately into Don Bosco's face.

"Since you won't take anything else, my good fellow," said the latter, "you may as well take leave."

He obeyed, and a boy let him out. The reason of this visit was soon explained. Don Bosco would have returned home late that evening, had not the Marquis Fassati brought him in his carriage much earlier than usual: and Grigio, probably, wanted to make sure that the Father was really safe at home.

In the autumn of 1866, Don Bosco again saw his faithful guardian. He was at Murialdo di Castelnuovo, and going to the house of a friend living at Moncucco. Night had come on, and the woods he had to pass through were by no means free from dangers. "Ah!" he said, "if only my good Grigio were here!" and, to his amazement, he saw him quietly walking by his side. The dog proved of immense service in defending him against the attacks of two savage mastiffs, set to guard the vines. On reaching his friend's house, the guests exclaimed at the beauty of the dog, and offered him various delicacies, all of which he declined. Some young clerics, puzzled at his refusal, shut him in a room, saying that, " when he had fasted twelve hours he would certainly eat or drink;" but when they went to liberate their captive in the morning he was gone.

No one has yet found out where this dog came from, or whither he has gone when his task for the time being was accomplished; he has remained unknown in the country, and, moreover, the following account, given by Dr. d'Espiney, makes him, after a disappearance of seventeen years, turn up again quite recently. " On the 12th of February, 1883," he tells us, " Don Bosco, accompanied by Don Durando, one of his priests, arrived at the Bordighiera station by the last train. He was not expected,

and there was no one to meet him. The
Salesian establishment, to which he was
going, is at some distance from the town;
he had only gone thither by daylight,
and in a conveyance, and did not well
know the way. The night was cloudy
and very dark, and the roads, after some
days of rain, extremely muddy. However, the travellers resolutely set out,
and got on pretty well, until, after they
had left behind them the last houses of
the town, they found it difficult to distinguish one object from another, and
lost their way. Presently, Don Bosco
found himself up to the knees in water:
his companion uttered an exclamation of
distress, but his alarm redoubled at the
sight of a huge dog which gambolled
around them, expressing by short barks
his friendly satisfaction. Don Bosco
joyfully recognised his faithful Grigio,
and resolved to trust him to get them
back into the right road; this he soon
accomplished, and did not leave them
until they had reached their destina-
tion.

* *
*

This may be the place to relate an incident, the precise date of which we have been unable to ascertain.

Don Bosco, in returning from one of his charitable expeditions outside the walls of Turin, was passing through a lonesome wood at nightfall, when an armed man emerged from the brushwood and demanded his purse or his life.

"As for my purse," said Don Bosco, calmly, " I have not got one: as for my life, no one can take it without the permission of God, who gave it."

"Come, come, *Abale!* no parleying; your purse, or I strike!"

At this moment, Don Bosco recognised in his aggressor one of the young culprits he had formerly catechised in the prisons of Turin.

"Beppo! can it indeed be you? Is this how you keep your promises? I trusted you so much, and now you have taken to such a disreputable trade as this!"

The robber had also, on his side, recognised the priest he had threatened, and now hung his head, ashamed.

" If only I had thought it could be you, Father, you may be very sure that you would never have been molested ! "

" That is not enough, my child : you must positively change your life; you are wearying the goodness and patience of God, and how do you know whether He will give you time for repentance at the hour of death ?"

" Certainly, Father. I will change my life : I promise you I will."

" And you must make your confession."

" Yes; I will make it."

" And when ?"

" Oh, shortly."

" Then make it now; that is best. Kneel down there, my child."

And, seating himself on a large stone, Don Bosco pointed to a place on the ground beside him. After some hesitation, the other fell on his knees, the priest passed an arm around his neck, as in former days, and heard his confession. Then, embracing his recovered penitent, he gave him a medal of Our Lady, Help of Christians, and the little money he

had in his pocket, after which, in company with his robber who escorted him
to the town gates, he returned to Turin.
He had saved the man, who became
thenceforward a thoroughly well-con-
ducted character.

* *
*

And now, after this somewhat lengthy
digression, for which, perhaps, some
apology is due, we resume the thread of
the narrative.

In 1849, the trials of the preceding
year were repeated, with little intermis-
sion. An increasing spirit of insubordi-
nation and revolution was abroad ; but
this, to Don Bosco, was only an addi-
tional incentive to strain every nerve to
rescue the young from its pernicious
influence. He now founded at Turin, a
third Salesian Oratory, that of " *The
Angel Guardian,*" in the quarter called
Vanchiglia, then very poor, and without
a church.   Later on, the Marchesa
Giulia Barolo built the Church of Santa
Giulia ; and a parish was formed out of
that quarter. In this same year also,
Don Bosco had the joy of seeing four of

his children of the Oratory enter Holy
Orders : they were the first-fruits of that
institution of St. Francis of Sales, which
was afterwards to have so rapid and
vigorous a development.

Don Bosco had, as we have seen,
rented by degrees the whole of Pinardi's
house. In 1851, his wish to purchase it
was unexpectedly realised. One day,
Pinardi said, half jestingly, to his tenant,
" Well, then, Don Bosco will not buy my
house ?"

" Don Bosco will buy it, when Signor
Pinardi asks a reasonable price."

" I have said 80,000 francs."

" Then let us say no more about it."

" But have you any offer to make ?"

" It is valued at 26,000 or 28,000
francs ; I will give you 30,000."

" And 500 francs to my wife, for
pins ?"

" As you please."

" You would give the money down, at
a single payment, within a fortnight ?
A thousand francs to be forfeited by
either party failing to keep to his con-
tract ?"

"Agreed!" They touched hands; it had not taken three minutes to conclude the bargain.

Don Bosco had not at that moment a single crown towards the required sum; but this was a matter in which the good of his children was concerned, and he had the fullest certainty that the money would be forthcoming.

In fact, no sooner had Pinardi left him than Don Cafasso came in, bringing him a donation of 10,000 francs from the Contessa Casazza Ricardi. Next day, a Rosminian Father went to consult Don Bosco on the use to which he should apply a sum of 20,000 francs, placed in his hands for any purpose he might choose. Nothing was more simple. Cotta, the banker, added 3,000 francs for the cost of transfer, and so this important transaction was completed; the money was paid, February 19, 1851, and Pinardi's house became the property of Don Bosco.

His next thought was to build a church, dedicated to St. Francis of Sales; the temporary building used as such being lower than the soil, damp, and ill ventilated, it not unfrequently happened that some of the children fainted for want of sufficient air.

The plan was drawn by M. Blachier, the architect, and the digging for the foundations at once began. There was the same total absence of funds, but also the same evident interposition of Divine Providence in supplying them. An unexpected gift from Victor Emmanuel, numerous smaller donations, and, lastly, a lottery, produced the required sum.

The church was consecrated on the 20th of January, 1852. Many of those present called to mind some words spoken by Don Bosco five years before, and which had been scarcely heeded at the time. When, in 1846, the workmen were digging out the ground of the shed which was to form the chapel, the boys amused themselves by running up and down the heaps of earth thrown outside. One Sunday Don Bosco mounted with them one of these heaps, and made them sing with him several times the words, " Praised for ever be the Name of Jesus

and the name of Mary; praised for
ever be the Name of Jesus, the Incar-
nate Word." Then he said: "My children, on this very spot where we are
standing will be one day the altar of a
beautiful church: here you will kneel to
receive Holy Communion, and here you
will sing the praises of God." Five
years had passed, and the high altar of
the Church of St. Francis of Sales occupied the spot he had indicated.

Some months afterwards the cholera
broke out at Turin, spreading conster-
nation in the city. As always, the poor-
est quarters suffered most, and the Oratory of the Valdocco was surrounded by
dead and dying.

The hospitals becoming quickly overcrowded, lazarets were formed, but the
great difficulty was to find persons willing to tend the sick. Don Bosco, with
several of the priests who assisted him,
had, from the first, hastened to attend
upon the sufferers. Then, seeing how
widespread and increasing was the terrible malady, he did not hesitate to
appeal to his children, expressing a wish

to see some of them help in this work of
mercy. Fourteen boys immediately
gave their names, and, a few days afterwards, thirty more. Day and night they
placed themselves at the disposal of those
in need of help, performing, with the
greatest care and attention, all the functions of infirmarians. Many of the sufferers in the Valdocco being in a state
of the utmost destitution, Mme. Margherita emptied one by one every linen
cupboard in the house to supply the
necessities of these poor creatures. One
day a boy ran in to beg another sheet,
having found a poor cholera-stricken
man lying on a most miserable pallet.
The charitable Margherita hunted every
corner in vain, all having been stripped,
when she caught sight of a table-cloth,
escaped, no one knew how, from the
general distribution. " Take this, my
boy ; it is the last in the house." And
the lad ran off with it, exulting, and carefully wrapped his poor patient in this
precious linen.

Not one of the Oratory boys was
attacked by the cholera, although latterly

they had ceased to take any of the pre-
cautions recommended. It is true that
when the epidemic began, Don Bosco
had offered his life for the lives of his
children. God did not accept this
offering of the shepherd, but He pro-
tected his youthful flock.

The Church of St. Francis of Sales
being completed, Don Bosco lost no time
in beginning the long-projected home
for his children. When about half
built, this narrowly escaped destruction
from the explosion of a powder mill,
about a quarter of a mile distant. Masses
of masonry and burning beams were
thrown into the court, and some of the
walls were much injured. It seemed
marvellous that the newly-erected church
should have escaped without harm.

The damaged building was repaired,
and approaching completion, when the
new walls, soaked by heavy and long-
continued rain, and injured by floods, as
well as weakened probably more than
had been perceptible by the effects of
the explosion, fell in with a crash.

This was on the 3rd of December,

1852. Next day the architect, examining an enormous pilaster, leaning dangerously over a frail tenement beneath, asked if the latter had been occupied the previous night. "I slept there," said Don Bosco, "with thirty of my children." "Then," said the man, "you may thank the Blessed Virgin that you are alive, for it seems to me a miracle that you were not all crushed to death."

Don Bosco, in no way discouraged by the double disaster this house had met with, set to work anew and finished it the following year. But his joy at seeing its completion was overshadowed by the greatest sorrow of his life—the loss of his admirable mother. She was attacked by inflammation of the lungs, brought on, in all probability, from over-work and exposure to damp, in the new building. From the first, there was little hope. The boys, in the greatest distress, redoubled their prayers and mortifications, to obtain her recovery; but such was not the will of God. She died on the 25th of November, the Feast of St. Catherine, in the arms of her son, after receiving all the last sacraments of the Church. No sooner had she passed away than Don Bosco, the tears streaming down his cheeks, hastened from the beloved dead to offer the Most Holy Sacrifice for the repose of her soul. This being done, he knelt and prayed before the image of our Blessed Lady : " Oh, Mother of Mercy ! my children and I have no longer a mother upon earth, do thou, therefore, more than ever, show thyself a Mother to us all ! "

The funeral of Mme. Margherita was one of the most touching sights imaginable : all her adopted children were there : the utmost order was observed, but the grief of these poor lads moved to tears all who saw them.

Don Bosco's prayer to the Mother of Mercy was not in vain. The growth of his work became more remarkable than ever. Large additions were made to the Oratory, partly by purchase, partly by building (in 1860-1863) ; and if the house of Valdocco, as it now exists, cannot boast perfect regularity as a building, it, nevertheless, fully realises in every particular the famous plan of which the mere description had brought Don Bosco under suspicion of insanity.

At the present moment this Oratory has sleeping room for a thousand persons, exclusive of pupils who attend during the day, or come to the evening classes. Large workshops are attached, where all the more useful and necessary trades are taught ; there are departments for carpenters, smiths, tailors, shoemakers, bakers, bookbinders, &c. The printing establishment is especially important. This, in 1883, had already issued more than two hundred different works, chiefly religious or educational. Adjoining it is a foundry for types, machinery for glazing paper, establishments for photography and phototypes, everything, in fact, that is required for the production of books and even of fine editions.

The boys are divided into two principal categories—artisans and students. The latter, who are of higher class and superior intelligence, were more particularly under the personal training of

Don Bosco, until their numbers so greatly increased that he was obliged to send them to Professor Giuseppe Bonanzino and Don Matteo Picco, both of whom opened classes gratuitously for Don Bosco's pupils. In this manner, numbers of young men have received an excellent education, and have gone out into the world as professors, doctors, schoolmasters, lawyers, or civil servants, &c., while a large number have entered Holy Orders : they have not only furnished the Salesian houses with priests and teachers, but the dioceses of Northern Italy have been supplied with some hundreds of these earnest men.

In order to give stability to his work, Don Bosco was desirous of forming a society of priests trained on his own system, who should carry on his institutions after his death. "Strangely enough, while he was deliberating how best to carry out this idea, he was sent for by the Minister Ratazzi, who made him a similar suggestion, assuring him that the Government would put no obstacle in the way. Yet this was the very minister who, with Cavour, had brought about the suppression of the religious orders in Italy."* Don Bosco took counsel on the matter with Archbishop Franzoni, who warmly encouraged the idea, advising him to go to Rome and lay his proposal at the feet of the Holy Father. The Pope, who, from the first, had appreciated Don Bosco and his work, received him with marked affection, approved of his plans, and commanded him to put them into execution without delay. And thus the Salesian Society was authoritatively founded by His Holiness Pius IX.

There are now seventeen Salesian houses in different parts of Italy, four in France, three in Spain, and twelve in South America. In these houses are more than 100,000 children, and over 6,000 priests are labouring amongst them. Besides this, in Patagonia some thousands of savages have been baptised. A Congregation of Sisters, called

* We are here quoting from the article on "Don Bosco," by Lady Herbert of Lea, in the *Month* for January, 1884.

"*Daughters of Mary, Help of Christians,*"
and intended to teach poor girls, has
also been founded.

When we consider all that has been
accomplished by Don Bosco within so
comparatively short a time, we are
struck with amazement, and compelled
to own that full of wonders is that simple
and perfect way which consists in utter
self-abandonment, without restriction or
reservation, to God and the work of God.
It might, however, be supposed by some
that Don Bosco is venturesome and even
rash in his undertakings, but this is not
the case. He does not begin a foundation unless circumstances clearly show
that it is called for ; but, once convinced
that it is right to begin, nothing stops
him, want of means or anything else.
And his method is very simple. "One
must begin," he says, "by taking the
burden on one's own shoulders, and the
further we go, the more we get accustomed to it." He always begins very
humbly : everything about the new foundation is poor and small ; a roof, and
bread, this is all he is anxious to secure

as a commencement, for his children and his priests, knowing that matters will improve as time goes on. "I once said to one of these priests," writes Dr. Espiney, "' But, Father, how do you manage to feed all these children?' I shall never forget the surprise with which he looked at me. 'How?' he said; 'Divine Providence feeds them!'" And this imperturbable faith that God will provide for the needs of his little ones, is graven in the heart of every Salesian priest.

Don Bosco never enlarges a house until it becomes too small to receive all who come: then he makes the requisite additions, in the certainty that, as these have become indispensable, the money to pay for them will come. But the inmates, so to speak, always come before the building; the house does not wait for them, but they for the house. He possesses, in a marked degree, the gift of organisation, as also of administration; and takes thought for the smallest details of each of his establishments. He is thoroughly acquainted with his priests, professors, and students, and

also has a distinct knowledge of every
one of the boys with whom he has had
to do; moreover, he never forgets any
face that he has seen, or any person
with whom he has spoken, no matter
how brief or unimportant the occasion
may have been.

His memory is prodigious. It is related of him that, when at the seminary,
he never bought a treatise on theology,
since, after hearing the theological lec-
tures, he could repeat them word for
word: it was the same with anything he
read, and in this way, by once reading
it, he learned by heart the whole of Rôhr-
bacher's Ecclesiastical History. He can
still recite entire cantos of Virgil and
Dante; and if a line is quoted, can always
continue the quotation. These unusual
gifts explain how it comes to pass that
he, who was a shepherd lad until the age
of fifteen, has been able to lay in so solid
a store of knowledge.

It is marvellous how, with weak health,
weak sight, and weak limbs, he can daily
get through an amount of work that is
simply enormous. Besides the direction

of his numerous houses, he is always ready to hear and comfort those who come to him, and their number is incredible: he also receives, on an average, two hundred letters a day. He has made it an invariable rule to do everything that comes before him as well as he possibly can, and without any hurry: in this he acts on the maxim of the celebrated Dr. Nelaton, who, when about to perform some difficult operation, would say to his assistants: "Above all, we must not hurry, for there is no time to be lost." Naturally impetuous and quick tempered, he has obtained so complete a mastery over himself, that nothing seems to have any power to disturb his calmness and equanimity. If you go to see him (and nothing is easier than to get admission), he receives you with all courtesy, as an honoured guest, and, although many abuse his kindness by making unreasonable demands upon his precious moments, he never, by word or sign, shows that his patience is tried, but treats them as if he had nothing to

As a rule, in all the Salesian Oratories the priests, professors, teachers, and master-workmen are Salesians, although, should it be advisable, special professors from without are called in. The methods of teaching invented by Don Bosco are said to be as remarkable for simplicity as for effectiveness, and are adopted on this account in many schools external to the Oratorians. With regard to the moral training, Don Bosco has invariably adopted the *preventive* method, which, by removing, as much as possible, opportunities for faults, removes also the necessity of punishment. His rule is essentially the rule of love, his first care to win the child's heart; when this is secured, a word of sorrow, or even a look, will suffice, and other punishments are useless.

In accordance with the ancient custom of the Church, the boys are allowed to make their First Communion at an early age: most of them receive Holy Communion every week. "Only by frequent confession and Communion, and daily attendance at Mass." wrote Don Bosco.

"can the foundations of true education be laid; and only thus can threats and punishments be rendered unnecessary."

The boys are as little as possible left to themselves. The Fathers are present at the studies, in the workshops, and, during recreation time, join the boys in their games. In the Salesian Oratory they do not play, any more than they work, by halves: even to watch the heartiness of their sports is an enjoyment. Formerly Don Bosco joined in the games, with wonderful alacrity and spirit. He is devotedly fond of children, and the boys are not slow in returning his attachment. When they come to him they always kiss his hands, and as they do so it is touching to see how their faces beam with affection.

From time to time during the day, but chiefly in the evening, when the day's work is over, a few cheering words are spoken to encourage the lads in a love of labour, and also in a high esteem for it, as having been sanctified and made honourable by our Lord and Saviour, who chose in his mortal life to be a lowly

working man.   This Divine Example
is ever set before them as their pattern
here below, and hereafter, when the toils
and trials of this life are over, as their
"exceeding great Reward" in the life
of the world to come.

"When Lord Palmerston went to
Valdocco"* (we quote the account
given by Lady Herbert of Lea), "he
called on Don Bosco simply as an
English stranger, without giving his
name. He examined all the workshops,
talked with the children, and, after the
simple dinner to which Don Bosco had
invited him, asked 'how he managed a
thousand boys without any punishment?'
Don Bosco smiled and said, 'Stay with
us till evening, and you will see.' Lord
Palmerston stayed, and went into the
chapel, where, after the evening recreation, the boys had all assembled, and
then he heard Don Bosco speak to them.
He listened to their simple and volun-
tary confession of the faults of the day,
and Don Bosco's words of counsel and

* See "Don Bosco," by Lady Herbert of Lea,
in the *Month* for January, 1884.

loving encouragement to each, and when he came out he wrung Don Bosco's hands, saying, 'Now I understand. You have won all their hearts, and so you can mould them as you please.' Then he gave his name, and said that 'for the first time he had learned what love could do with rough and untaught natures.'"

Very many of these boys, now grown to manhood, have made themselves honourable positions in the world; but, all alike, whether in higher or humbler careers of life, preserve a warm attachment to the hospitable house where they were brought up. All to whom it is possible return once a year to make a retreat; and they regard Don Bosco, and others, their former masters, with the most affectionate and reverent gratitude.

One day, in Rome, Don Bosco, with his secretary, was walking along the Corso, when he was accosted by a colonel in full dress : " *Signor Abate,* are you not Don Bosco?" . . .

No sooner was the answer given than

the soldier, then and there, dropped on his knees, seized and kissed the priest's hands, exclaiming: " O my dear, good Father!"

" But, my dear colonel, what are you thinking of? what do you mean ?"

" Dear Father, don't you remember the poor little orphan you found in the street at ——, and took home with you, and to whom you were for six years both father and mother?"

"What! then is it you, my little *gamin?* You seem to have got on fairly well in the world."

"Yes: when I left the Patronage I enlisted, and, thanks to what I had learned there, I was promoted, until now I am colonel."

He would not let Don Bosco go without promising to dine with him next day, when he presented his young wife and three beautiful children. The good priest's heart rejoiced to see the happy home which Divine Providence had granted to one of his poor orphans. This incident is, however, of recent date: we must now go back nearly twenty years.

When our Holy Father Pius IX. was informed of Don Bosco's wish to build a church in honour of *Our Lady, Help of Christians,* he remarked that this dedication would assuredly draw down many graces from the Queen of Heaven. His Holiness sent his special benediction to the work, and also a donation of 500 francs. The Holy Father's remark has been repeatedly verified, 'for it is in connection with this foundation that, in full submission to the judgment of the Church in regard to them, we have to mention certain extraordinary favours granted in answer to prayer, through Our Lady's intercession—favours which became manifest from the time this building was begun.

No sooner had Don Bosco received the Pope's approval than he fixed upon a suitable site, close by the Oratory of Valdocco. The plan of the structure was in the form of a Latin cross, covering an area of about 1,500 square yards.

When the first stone of the Church of Our Lady, Help of Christians, was laid

times, or four pence, in his pocket. The
500 francs sent by the Holy Father had
gone towards defraying the price of the
ground.   The municipality, and also
several private persons, had promised
donations; but, under one pretext or
another, these engagements were not
kept at the time.   Don Bosco, however,
set the men to dig the foundations.   At
the end of a 'fortnight he owed them
1,000 francs; and these poor men could
not be kept waiting for their money.

A few days previously he had had
occasion, in the exercise of his ministry,
to visit a lady, who, for three months,
had been confined to her bed, and was
reduced by fever and incessant coughing
to the last extremity of weakness.

" O Father," she said, " how thankful I should be, if only I had strength to
take even a few steps in my room !"

According to his custom, Don Bosco
advised her to make a novena to Our
Lady, Help of Christians, and say with
all her heart, three times a day, the
Pater, Ave, Gloria, and *Salve Regina.*

It was now the eighth day of the

novena, and Don Bosco went to inquire after the sick lady's progress. The maid, who opened the door, told him joyfully that her mistress was cured, and had been twice to the church to return thanks for her recovery. While she was speaking, the lady entered :

"O Father!" she exclaimed, "I am perfectly cured; I have already been to thank Our Blessed Lady for the grace she has obtained for me, and I wish, also, to make an offering for the Church you are building in her honour: it is my first, but, assuredly, it shall not be my last."

So saying, she put a small, but weighty parcel into his hands. When, on returning home, he opened it, he found that it contained fifty gold Napoleons.

And thus the 1,000 francs of which he was in need that day might truly be said to fall, as it were, directly from the hand of Mary, Help of Christians.

Don Bosco kept silence on this occurrence, but not so the lady who was cured. The news spread rapidly, and produced an extraordinary thrill of devotion to Our Blessed Lady under this, one of her dearest titles. Multitudes of persons made novenas to Mary, Help of Christians, promising, if their petitions were granted, to make offerings to her church. In fact, so abundant were the gifts and thank-offerings that this magnificent church was built without a single collection being made: the sums required towards the cost of its erection always came in unsought-for, except by prayer, and almost invariably at the moment when they were urgently wanted.

The total cost of the building amounted to rather over a million francs, and a carefully kept register of the receipts and expenditure proves that of this sum, 85,000 francs consisted of the thank-offerings of persons who had received signal answers to prayer; and thus each stone of the edifice is, as it were, a testimony which proves that it is most pleasing to Our Divine Lord to grant the petitions He receives through the hands of his Immaculate Mother. Moreover, numerous thank-offerings were given in the form of sacred vessels and vestments for the service of the altar, as also lamps, statues, paintings, and other objects for the adornment of the sanctuary. The church was consecrated on the 9th of June, 1868: the feast of dedication, which continued for eight days, attracting an immense concourse of people.

As we have seen, it was in connection with the commencement of this church that first took place the remarkable cures which, it is said, have subsequently increased in number. Upon the character of these cures the Church alone can pronounce with authority; nevertheless, subject to her infallible judgment with regard to them, we will mention a few of the instances in which the hand of God seems to be plainly discernible.

One Saturday in May, 1869, a peasant girl, named Maria Stardero, from Vinovo, came with her aunt and another woman into the Church of Mary, Help of Christians. Two years previously a violent inflammation in the eyes had gradually destroyed the sight, and for more than a year she had been perfectly blind. She then resolved to make this pilgrimage. After praying at the altar of Our Lady, the women asked to speak to Don Bosco, and were taken to the sacristy. When he had heard their story, he asked what the doctors said of the case.

" They say that the eyes are partially destroyed, and that the girl is blind for life," said the aunt.

"Can you distinguish large objects from small ones ?" asked Don Bosco.

" Alas ! Father, I can distinguish nothing."

Bidding the aunt remove the black bandage, he placed the girl facing a window.

" Now, cannot you see this bright light?"

" No ; I can only see darkness."

" And you wish to see ?"

" Wish it, Father? yes, more than anything in the world! I am a poor girl, and ought to work for my living."

" Would you use your eyes for the good of your soul, and not to offend God ?"

"Yes; I promise with all my heart. But my lot is very hard!" and she burst into tears.

"Have confidence in Our Blessed Lady, and she will help you."

"I hope she will; but meantime I am blind."

"To the glory of God, and of the Blessed Virgin Mary, tell me, what am I holding in my hand?"

Making an effort, and fixing her eyes steadily, Maria exclaimed: "I can see! It is a medal of Our Lady!"

"And on the other side is —— ?"

"An aged man, with a flowering rod in his hand; it is St. Joseph."

"*Madonna Sanctissima!*" cried the aunt, "then it is true; you can indeed see!"

"Yes, thanks be to God; the Blessed Virgin has obtained for me this favour!" and she held out her hand for the medal, which, falling on the floor, rolled into a dark corner of the sacristy.

The aunt was about to pick it up, but Don Bosco stopped her.

"Leave it," he said; "let us see

if Our Blessed Lady has obtained a perfect cure."

The girl found it immediately, and then, almost beside herself with joy, started in all haste to go back to Vinovo, even forgetting, in her eagerness, first to make her thanksgiving in the church. Nevertheless, she very soon returned, and with her the aunt, who, at the very time of her niece's cure, had been suddenly and entirely freed from severe rheumatism of long standing.

A certain doctor of Turin, high in his profession, hearing of various cases of this kind, which although out of the common order of things, he had reason to consider authentic, one day presented himself at the Oratory of St. Francis of Sales, and asked for Don Bosco.

"I am told, Father, that you cure all sorts of complaints."

"I ? Nothing of the kind!"

"But I can mention the names of persons cured, and the nature of their maladies."

"Many people come here, asking fa-

vours by the intercession of Our Lady,
Help of Christians : and if, after a tri-
duum or a novena, the cure they ask for
is granted, it is she alone who has obtained it for them ; I am simply nothing
at all in the matter."

" Well, then, let her cure me, and I
will believe in these miracles of hers. I
suffer from epileptic fits, and these have
become so violent that for a year past I
never dare to go out alone. Now, what
am I to do ?"

" The same that other people do :
kneel down and pray with me; prepare
to cleanse and strengthen your soul by
confession and communion, and see if
the Blessed Virgin does not relieve
you."

" Bid me do something else instead,
for this I cannot do ! "

" And why not ?"

" Because it would be hypocrisy on my
part; I do not believe in God, nor in the
Virgin Mary, nor in miracles, nor in
prayer !"

For a moment Don Bosco was silent

the Holy Spirit he spoke to his visitor words of so much earnestness and sweetness and penetrating power, that presently the doctor knelt down and made the sign of the cross.

"I am surprised to find that I remember how to make it," he said, "for it is now forty years since I left it off." He no longer refused to pray, and afterwards remained to make his confession.

When he rose from his knees he felt within himself that he was cured.

From that moment he has had no return of his malady, and has many a time come to the sanctuary of Our Blessed Lady to thank her for healing him in body and soul.

Some of these cures have been the germ of far-spreading and very important results in the spiritual order, as in the case of the one we will next relate.

In the town of San Pietro d'Arena, a few years ago, religion had sunk almost to the lowest ebb; the church was well nigh deserted, and the one priest did not find full occupation for his time among all this population of 30,000 souls. Three Masonic lodges had things all their own way ; their detestable influence paralysed that of the priest, and destroyed all the germs of good among his people.

The wife of a railway clerk of this town fell dangerously ill. She was the mother of five children. The doctors having pronounced her case hopeless, the priest proposed to administer the last sacraments. The woman, who was not a very devout Christian, demurred to this, and declared that she would make her confession to nobody but Don Bosco. Thankful at her willingness to make it at all, the parish priest immediately wrote to Don Bosco, who came without delay. He was at that very time meditating the foundation of a house at San Pietro, and waiting for some opening by which Divine Providence would enable him to carry out his wishes.

The sick woman showed great satisfaction when Don Bosco entered her room. He spoke to her encouragingly, and then heard her confession. But instead of proceeding afterwards to

give her the Holy Viaticum, he said:
"With regard to your Communion, we
shall be more at our ease in the
church. I am here for some days: I
am going to pray, and to set my children also to pray for you ; and I will say
Mass for your intention. Come to my
Mass some morning soon, and I will give
you Holy Communion."

The husband, at these words, could
not repress a murmur of surprise and in-
dignation. "Impossible!" he exclaimed,
"this is no time for jesting! You see
that this woman is dying, helpless to rise
from her bed, and you can talk to her of
going to church!"

"Our Lady, Help of Christians, can
obtain for us all that she wishes," said
Don Bosco, calmly. "Let us, all together, pray to her." And he knelt down,
the husband following his example (to
the wonder of those present), and recited
the *Pater*, *Ave*, *Gloria*, and *Salve Regina*.

"You must says these prayers very
regularly until Christmas, without fail,"
he added (it was then the 6th of December, 1872), and he passed a medal round

the neck of the sick woman, gave one also to her husband, and left the house.

Immediately this woman felt a change come over her; all pain was gone, and every trace of fever. She was completely cured.

A day or two afterwards she and her husband were, early in the morning, at church, returning fervent thanks for the immense favour granted them. The wife received Holy Communion from the hands of Don Bosco, and the impression made on the husband by what he had witnessed resulted in his thorough conversion. He often repeated that the coming of this holy priest had not only been the means of restoring his wife to health, but also of restoring peace to his soul.

All the town was moved by the fact of this cure; it produced an awakening which resulted in numberless conversions. The church was soon full again, and before long three more clergy found plenty of employment in helping the good parish priest, whose heart overflowed with joy.

Shortly afterwards a Salesian Oratory,

the Hospice of St. Vincent de Paul, was founded, and is flourishing in this town. A large church has since been built, also, in which ten Salesian priests are labouring for the good of souls. The church and hospice are in the centre of the three Masonic lodges—the standard of the King of kings raised in the midst of the army of revolt.

*
* *

Instead of making any attempt to classify the recorded cases of cures which appear to have, more or less, a supernatural character, we prefer to take them in the order of time, gleaning one here and there in such a way as to show their continued recurrence.

*
* *

On the 4th of June, 1874, when, early in the morning, the doors of the church of Mary, Help of Christians, at Turin, were opened, a poor man, bent nearly double, lay on the ground before the middle entrance. Being asked why he was there, he said he had come to ask without difficulty, assisted to the sacristy, his spine and limbs being so much contracted as to render him almost helpless, even with the aid of a stout crutch.

That day was the great Feast of Corpus Christi. All the priests were engaged either at the altar or in the confessionals, until, about eight o'clock, Don Bosco entered the sacristy. After hearing the man's account of his state, which, moreover, was self-evident, Don Bosco asked how he had managed to get there.

"A neighbour, who was coming this way last night, brought me in his cart, and left me at the church door. The doctors said they could do nothing for me, and so my relations and the priest of my parish advised me to ask Our Lady, Help of Christians, to obtain for me what she has obtained for so many others."

"Kneel down, my good man," said Don Bosco. The man could only obey by the aid of those who stood by; his hands as well as his feet were contracted and rigid.

Don Bosco gave him his blessing, and then said: "If you have faith in God's mercy, and the power of Our Lady's intercession, stretch out your hand."

"I cannot!"

"Yes, you can. Begin by the thumb."

He tried, and succeeded. "Now, the forefinger." He did so, and thus, one by one, with all the fingers; then, beaming with joy, he made a great sign of the cross. "Yes, the holy Madonna has obtained this for me!"

"If so, give glory to God by standing on your feet."

The man reached out a hand for his crutch.

"No," said Don Bosco, "you must show your confidence by standing up by yourself."

And he did so. The curvature of the spine had disappeared, as well as the contraction of the limbs. He stretched himself to his full height, and took long strides up and down the sacristy.

"My friend, in token of your gratitude, go and make a genuflexion before the altar of the Blessed Sacrament." He obeyed, and returning, fervently gave thanks aloud to God and Our Blessed Lady.

" And now promise me that you will have a great devotion to the Holy Virgin, and lead the life of a good Christian."

"I promise it; and next Sunday I will go to confession and communion." So saying, the man took up his crutch, carried it aloft, as if presenting arms, and gravely marched out of the church, and back to his parish.

***

In the next instance to be related, a vocation to the priesthood was decided by the sight of a cure which took place on the 23rd of May, 1877.

Charles Albert, Count of Giletta and Casella, former member of the Subalpine Parliament, and one of the highest among the old nobility of Piedmont, was a man of well-known piety, full of good works, and of great love for the poor. He was a widower, and, after the marriage of his only son, desired to devote himself for the remainder of his life in some more special manner to the service of God. He consulted Don Bosco as to the form his decision should take, and was told by him to become a Salesian priest.

He had, it is true, felt himself drawn to
the priesthood, but, besides being held
back by motives of humility, it seemed
to him that, to begin to prepare for it by
the necessary studies, at the age of 63,
was out of his power. Nevertheless, Don
Bosco's advice was still the same; and
the count by degrees became accustomed
to the idea, though inclined to doubt its
wisdom, and to suspect that a great desire to obtain priests for the Oratory
might partially obscure the judgment of
his adviser in this matter. In any case
he resolved to take time for consideration.

One morning—it was the day before
the Feast of Mary, Help of Christians—
he went, as it was his frequent custom,
to the Oratory, to see Don Bosco. He
found the ante-room already full of people
waiting their turn, and took his place near
the door, where his attention was immediately drawn to two of the persons near
him, a peasant woman and her daughter,
a girl of ten or eleven years old. The
child seemed to be in great suffering;
she was unable to stand, or even to sit
up, without being supported, and, in

spite of the mother's care, she fell an
inert mass to the right or the left, as she
was moved. After waiting some time, the
mother rose, and, with a deep sigh,
moved towards the door of exit, holding
her daughter up under the shoulders, as
the child's limbs bent helplessly under
her. Being asked why she was going
without having seen Don Bosco, she
answered: " Because my poor child suf-
fers too much ; besides, 1 am wanted at
home; I only want to ask Our Lady's
blessing for the child." Then she told
how her daughter, who was subject to
terrible convulsions, had, after one of
these attacks, remained paralysed and
speechless, unable for a month past to
articulate a word.

All present, touched with compassion,
agreed to let this poor sufferer pass before them. It was plain that nothing less
than a miracle could cure her, and with
this conviction, a sudden thought occurred to the Count of Giletta. After
lifting up his heart to God, he besought
Our Lady to let this child's cure be to
him a sign that he should enter the

priesthood, resolving, should not this be granted, to think of it no more.

A few moments afterwards, mother and child entered Don Bosco's room. The girl was laid upon a couch. After hearing what the mother had to say, and bidding her have confidence in the mercy of God and the help of Mary, he bade her hold the child in a kneeling posture, and gave her the blessing of Our Lady, Help of Christians. He then bade her make the sign of the cross. She was about to make it with her left hand, which was not paralysed.

"No," insisted Don Bosco; "not with the left hand, but the right."

"She has no use in her right hand, Father."

"No matter! Now, my child, try."

The child raised the paralysed arm, and, with perfect ease, made the sign of the cross.

"Well done!" said Don Bosco. "You have made the sign of the cross very well indeed, but you did not pronounce the words. Now make it again, and say the words with me."

She did so, repeating the sacred words, " In the name of the Father, and of the Son, and of the Holy Ghost. Amen."

" Oh, mother !" she exclaimed, " Our Blessed Lady has cured me !"

On hearing her dumb child restored to speech, the mother burst into tears of joy.

" And now," continued Don Bosco, " make haste to thank Our Lady, and say the *Ave Maria* with all your heart."

The girl recited it distinctly, with great devotion ; after which Don Bosco, in order to ascertain if she had also recovered the use of her limbs, bade her rise from her knees and walk. She obeyed without the slightest difficulty, walked, and then ran round the room. Her step was firm and easy ; she was completely cured. In her joy she opened the door into the ante-room, and said to those who had compassionately let her, speechless and helpless, pass before them.

" Help me to thank Our Blessed Lady. See, she has cured me ; I can use my hand ; I can walk ; there is nothing the matter with me any more !"

It is impossible to describe the emo-

tion produced by the sight of the cured
child, and the hearing of her glad words.
The people crowded round her with tear-
ful joy, and exclamations of wonder and
gratitude to God and the Blessed Virgin.
Don Bosco himself was so greatly im-
pressed by what had come to pass that he
trembled from head to foot. The rejoicing mother and child then went to make
their thanksgivings in the church.

The Count of Giletta was the most
deeply interested witness of all that had
occurred. The sign he had scarcely dared
to ask was given. " The Holy Virgin has
spoken," he said ; " I will be a Salesian
priest.'' And this resolution was further
confirmed some weeks later, when, meeting a young girl, who, with her parents,
was taking an offering to the church of
Mary, Help of Christians, he recognised
her as Giuseppina Longhi, the child who
had been so marvellously cured. Im-
pressed as he had been at the time, he
nevertheless had afterwards asked himself whether the cure, almost instanta-
neous as it was, could also be lasting ;
and this question had caused him consi-

derable uneasiness of mind. He rejoiced, therefore, at this unexpected meeting, and stopped to ask Giuseppina if she continued in good health.

"Yes," she said, "I am perfectly well. I can walk and talk, and write and learn my lessons as if I had never been ill."

"And only see," said the mother, "the fresh colour in her cheeks! and her appetite is excellent. All our neighbours agree that her cure is a miracle."*

But the Count needed no more assurances: he saw the child, and was satisfied.

*
* *

A year after the occurrence just related, namely, on the 24th of May, 1878, a young officer came in great distress to see Don Bosco at the Oratory. His wife had long been suffering from a cruel malady, and he had now been told that she had not much longer to live. Nevertheless, he had come to entreat Don Bosco to obtain from God the dying lady's recovery.

* Giuseppina Longhi is now one of the religious of Mary, Help of Christians. Don Charles Albert Cays de Giletta, Salesian priest, went to his re-

Don Bosco, after a few of the comfort-
ing and strengthening words he knows
so well how to speak, invited his visitor
to kneel and pray with him, according to
his invariable custom, and asking Our
Blessed Lady to aid them with her power-
ful intercession : then the officer took
leave. However, in an hour from his de-
parture he returned again, in all haste,
and asked for Don Bosco.

"Impossible at present," was the answer. "He is at this moment presiding
at a meeting of the benefactors of the
house, met on account of the festival of
to-day, and we cannot disturb him."

"Tell him my name, and say that I
have the greatest wish to see him for a
moment."

Don Bosco went at once to the officer,
whose face was now radiant with joy.

"Do you know, Father," he said, "that
while I was with you, my wife, whom I
had left in bed, and apparently near
death, ceased to suffer ; all her pains left
her, and she felt her strength return.
She insisted on dressing ; and when I
reached home she came to meet me. sav-

his pocket a rich gold bracelet: "This," he continued, "was a present I made my wife when we were married. With all our hearts we both offer it to Our Lady, Help of Christians, in token of our gratitude for the unhoped-for cure she has obtained for us."

Don Bosco returned to the assembly, and, showing the bracelet, related how he had just received it as a thank-offering for another cure obtained by Our Lady's intercession.

The following account is given by Lady Herbert of Lea:* After saying that, "over and over again Don Bosco has found himself without a farthing to pay his workmen or feed his children, and invariably, in answer to his prayers, the exact sum has arrived, often from the most unexpected quarters," she continues: "We will mention one instance known to ourselves, which has not, we believe, found a place as yet in any record of these marvels. A relation of ours, the Marquis S——, had, several years

* See *Month*, already referred to.

ago, lent a large sum of money to a
young man who was on the brink of ruin
from a gambling transaction. He lost
sight of the youth, never spoke of it to a
human being, and certainly never thought
he should ever see his money again. Two
years ago he was going through Turin,
on his way to the railway station, when
he met this very young man, who hastened to speak to him, and told him that
the lesson he had given him had not
been lost, that he had never touched a
card since, and that he had come back
to Turin on purpose to pay his debt,
which he proceeded to do, thrusting a
large sum into his hands. The Marquis
S—— proceeded to the station, and finding there that the hour of the train had
been changed (being the first of the
month), thought he would pay a visit to
Don Bosco, who lived close by. He
knocked at the door of his room, and was
going in, when, before he had time to say
'How do you do,' Don Bosco met him
with the words, 'I was expecting you.
I want you to give me the money you
have in your breast pocket,' mentioning

" The marquis exclaimed: 'How on earth could you know this? I received it most unexpectedly not ten minutes ago. Do you know young Count B——?'

" 'No,' replied Don Bosco; 'but I know you have the very sum I want to pay my workmen. You shall have it back in a week.'

" Too amazed to reply, the marquis handed him the money, for which Don Bosco gave him a receipt; and that very day week the exact sum was returned to him."

We cannot better conclude this part of our subject than by one more quotation (kindly permitted) from the same source:

" Last year (1883) at Rome, where, by desire of the Pope, he is building a large church and orphanage dedicated to the Sacred Heart, his clerk of the works came one day for the pay of the men. Don Bosco had only a few pence in his pocket, and told him so. Scarcely had the man,

Bosco, without opening it, recalled the clerk, and told him to see whether what he wanted was in the envelope, which he handed to him. The man did as he was bid, and found it contained bank-notes for £400, the exact sum required.

"'Another time you will have more faith,' was Don Bosco's sole comment, while he gratefully thanked the donor who had rendered him so signal a service. But these are only two instances of what is of daily occurrence. Don Bosco was anxious not long ago to get some English students, and asked us to send him any youths with vocations who had not means to prosecute their studies in England. We did so, and one youth who was sent, though an excellent fellow, had yet a thorough John Bull spirit of incredulity of anything new or out of the way. Yet he had not been there a year before he wrote to a good priest, who had been his director, saying : ' You know how disinclined I was to believe in any of the strange things I was told when I first came here. But seeing is believing, and man must be blind and a fool not to feel that he is indeed in presence of one who, if not a saint, is most singularly favoured by God, for he obtains all he prays for, whether it be for temporal means to carry on his great works, or the cure of physical and moral diseases, cures which he attributes entirely to the intercession of MARY, HELP OF CHRISTIANS.'"

Dr. d'Espiney states that, among all the thousands of boys brought up by the Salesian Fathers, not one has ever incurred judicial prosecution or penalty. Even had it not been so, it is an undeniable fact that the Salesian Society, solely occupied as it is in saving and educating poor and neglected children, renders immense service to every country in which it is planted. Every year 25,000 youths and young men leave these institutions fitted for the work of their life, and the same number of children enter, to receive the same care and training in their turn. From various countries Don Bosco receives requests to plant there fresh offshoots of his work, requests with which he cannot comply for want of resources priests and professors to meet these demands.

***

The chief works founded by Don Bosco are:

1. The Society of *Salesians* or *Salesian Oratorians;* consisting of some thousands of priests, missionaries, and lay professors and assistants.

2. The *Institute of Mary, Help of Christians*, for encouraging and maturing vocations to the priesthood, among the youths attending the Salesian Oratory.

3. The Institute of the *Daughters of Mary, Help of Christians*, chiefly for teaching poor girls.

4. *Salesian Co-operators*, men and women.

***

The Salesian foundations, as enumerated by Dr. d'Espiney, are:

In FRANCE, four: 1. The *Patronage de St. Pierre*, at Nice (1875). 2. Two agricultural orphanages of St. Joseph for boys, at Navarre, near La Crau d'Hyères; and 3, one for girls, St. Isidor, at Saint-Cyr, Var. 4. The Oratory of St. Léon, at Marseilles.

2. At Malaga.   3. One is in course of erection at Barcelona.

Besides numerous foundations already planted in South America, at Buenos Ayres, Montevideo, &c., &c.

**

The Association of Salesian Co-ope-RATORS, now numbering nearly 80,000 members, was first planned by Don Bosco as a regular institution in 1858. His rules for this association, after being more than once laid before his Holiness Pius IX., were completed and adopted in 1874.

The Holy Father not only gave his full and cordial approbation to the institution, but inscribed his own name at the head of the list of Co-operators.   Moreover, he erected this institution into a *Third Order*, with the power of gaining all the Indulgences which can be gained by Tertiaries of any Order soever, and in particular by the Tertiaries of St. Francis of Assisi.

All these privileges have been confirmed by our Holy Father Leo XIII., who. on inscribing his own name as Sale-

"Each time that you have to speak to your Co-operators, tell them that I bless them from my heart. The purpose of your society being to rescue the young from ruin, bid them unite, heart and soul, in aiding you to accomplish this purpose."

The Pope, at the same time (1879), appointed Cardinal Nina Protector of the Society. Its members may be enrolled from the age of sixteen. Their work is to assist the Salesian Fathers in seeking out destitute and neglected children ; to collect small sums towards their clothing and maintenance, and to aid in the distribution of Christian books. In fact, to help in all the ways within their power to check the progress of infidelity among the young, and keep them faithful to God and his Church, faithful to Christ, devout to his Blessed Mother, loyal to his Vicar, and thus to advance the kingdom of our Lord on earth.

M. H. Gill & Son, Printers, Dublin.

.

www.ingramcontent.com/pod-product-compliance
Lightning Source LLC
Chambersburg PA
CBHW030546270326
41927CB00008B/1541